Looking for Derek

Looking for Derek

Looking for Derek

David Banning

CHROMA EDITIONS

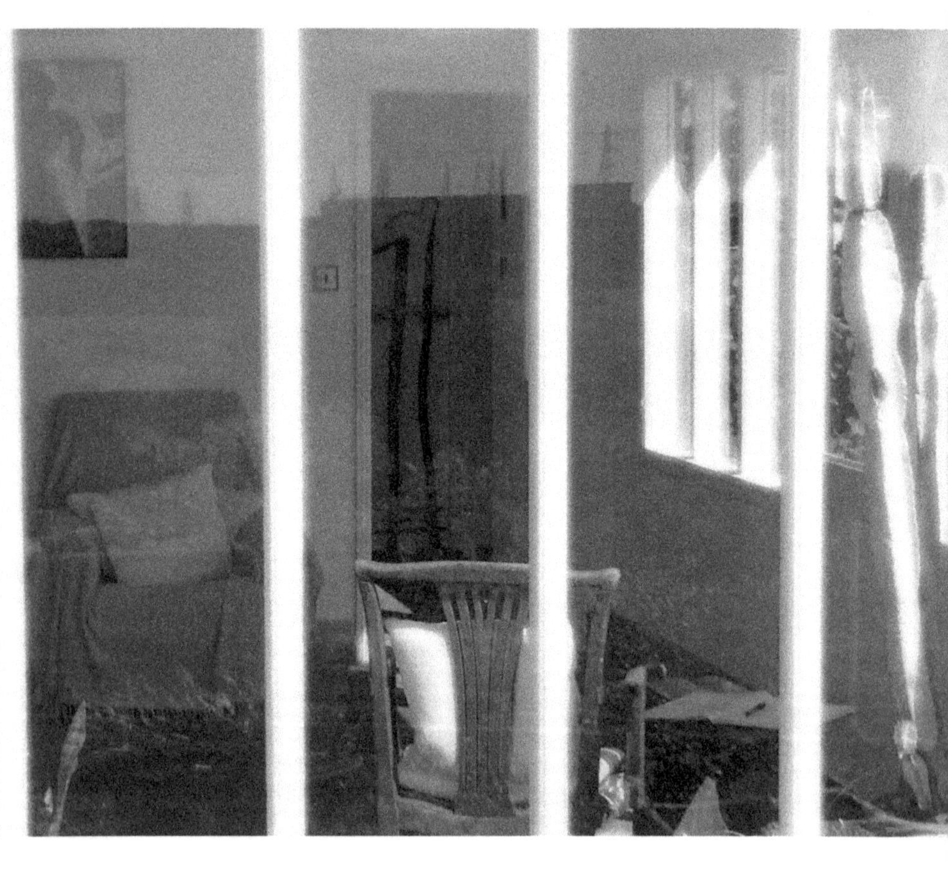

Notes - From *Modern Nature 17th October 1989:*
Derek meets Gen wheeling his daughter Jeunesse in a pram. Gen is dressed in a grey suit and dog collar with a golden Psychic TV cross on his lapel. He'd bought the outfit in Brighton and tells Derek it has made a world of difference and that he should definitely give it a go. People help him cross any busy streets with the child and even call him Sir…

January 1990…
Everyone called it 'porn alley.' You can find it at the narrower market-end of Berwick Street in Soho otherwise known as Walker's Court. I met Andy at a recording studio nearby during a short stint of work experience. Any downtime meant a quick pint or two surrounded by carved wooden panels and etched glass at the John Snow. Soon enough Andy offered me an opportunity as a Tape operator and general dogsbody at a studio opening round the corner. The perfect moment to be released from a childhood wrapped tight with forceful ambition and impatience. Lying side-by-side with the gold diggers of Wardour Street, Walker's Court had been the main focus of London's sex trade for 200 years. The new place was hidden from view on Blore Court, down a barely noticeable crack inbetween Berwick Street's tall buildings. Psychic TV led by Genesis P-Orridge became the first band to record at Andy's new venture 'The Beat Farm.' A self-appointed cultural engineer, Genesis or Gen liked to dress up in bishop garb and loiter in the neighbourhood. He'd hang around doorways plastered with handwritten signs offering the promise of 'models.' Up above sparkling neon lights tinted a motley fabric of concrete and dead beats. Gen had been wonderfully labelled a 'wrecker of civilisation' by a Tory MP for his part in the exhibition '*Prostitution*' staged at the ICA. Since then he'd gained a rep as someone who marked out the phantoms of

outsider culture and trampled over any cultural taboos. Fresh
with the possibilities of escape, I was introduced to him just
before sessions for the album *'Towards Thee Infinite Beat'* began.
He stood in the doorway of the studio kitchen dressed in a
long black cassock with a white linen over-garment and Roman
collar. Gen smiled and fixed me with a long gaze, "you've got
an arty face" he remarked. Other members of the band filed
in and reminisced about past events like the 'Psychic Rally in
Heaven.' Gen looked thoughtful for a moment until he re-
called one particular Saturday morning in September 1982. "I
picked up Derek from his place on Charing Cross Road before
we drove out to Heathrow to meet Burroughs. He'd brought
his Super-8 and filmed continuously after we'd whisked Bill
off to the Chelsea Arts Club." The footage turned into the
short film 'Pirate Tape' an experimental portrait that also featured a soundtrack by Gen's newly formed Psychic TV. "I gave
Derek £50 towards the cost of film because he was so skint.
He'd begun selling his clothes and books to pay rent!" I had
no idea who Gen was talking about at the time, but I could
easily empathise with the plight of a struggling filmmaker especially when faced with a similar financial meltdown myself.
Penniless and hungry, I had to sleep on the studio sofa after
long sessions finished in the early hours. Lying awake with the
noise of mind forged manacles permeating the streets outside,
I could barely imagine that some thirty years later I would
make a pilgrimage to the former home of the impoverished
film maker - Derek Jarman's Prospect Cottage…

Notes: *The name Dungeness derives from the Old English 'næs', meaning 'headland', the first part probably connected with the nearby Denge Marsh. A corruption of Danger Ness, the Headland of Danger - popular etymology attributes a French origin to the name, providing an interpretation as 'dangerous nose.'*

On the car radio at Warwick Services a Trump lawbreaker spewed out another round of unhinged horror. As I exited the Costa drive-thru my thoughts suddenly drifted to the character Aeon. The anti-hero of *Neutron* who set out into comparable bright sunshine dressed as a medieval pilgrim with a palmer's wide-brimmed hat and shepherd's staff. A trailer for the end of the world, the film was set around the empty shell of Battersea power station and the wasteland of the Berlin Wall. Work on the unreleased project commenced in 1979, not long after one of my favourite Jarman films *Jubilee* had been released. In his autobiography, *Dancing Ledge*, Jarman revealed that David Bowie and Steven Berkoff were originally cast to play the lead roles.

I drove further south into the hot glow of the South Downs. Into a sun bleached landscape where the dream treatment of mass-destruction shimmers through car windows. I watched a private message from Tilda Swinton on my phone at a campsite on the fringes of Brighton. She urged visitors to Prospect Cottage to dig really deep into the peace, resource and treasure of the so-called Tardis. Feel the power, look for hagstones and plug into the toolbox or battery. As I sat beside my tent eating sandwiches and crisps, a pink and violet sunset coloured the enormous sky above the race course near Woodingdean. After an hour or so with the light fading into black bands, the glowing dots of car headlights on the coast road brought a last swagger of boogie-woogie to the night. The following morning I awoke to clear blue skies. Before setting off I made last minute preparations for the drive to Dungeness. Fishing through my emails to dig out the important one from Creative Folkestone, (the newly appointed custodians of the cottage) to re-familiarise myself with the information surrounding timed visits.

The journey was supposed to take about an hour and a half. As expected, the A-road was mostly stop/start, stop/start on a busy Saturday morning. I wound down the windows and lapsed into a series of ghostly daydreams. Passing through village greens populated in part by refugees, ex-London retirees and brightly coloured bouncy castles. By the side of the road near Camber Sands a dead badger bled out into the world. Further on signs for the Channel Tunnel spoke of more failed boundaries amid crossings made by small boats. Intensifying debate about unauthorised migration and asylum seeking, the arrivals are often brought ashore onto the huge windswept spit at Dungeness by lifeboats from the RNLI. Despite predictable and inflammatory rhetoric about running a 'migrant taxi service', donations to the voluntary organisation hit unprecedented levels in 2021. Exposing the phantoms of the national psyche, now any questions about the reviled and marginalised are diverted straight to the Home Office. Once again the dead are transparent in a hostile culture which echoes back to Jarman, who battled similar assumptions after confirming his HIV+ status. I noticed another more playful sign at a junction next to a petrol station, 'Sheds for Sale – Free Erection!' Getting closer to Dungeness, the sun stayed with me all the way onto the tip of the Romney Marsh peninsula.

Suddenly the tall medieval tower of Lydd church, Jarman's 'cathedral of the marshes' came into view. The tide was out as I made my way slowly onto the bands of shingle. There it is I thought. Finally, after all these years, a passing shadow from the dark thunder clouds of memory. I got out of the car and knelt down, picked up a stone and stood for a long while in silent reflection. Perhaps I was hoping to participate in some form of consciousness, a vision that might resonate for years to come. Strangely, as I looked over the desolate landscape I envisaged visitors bustling round Wordsworth's Dove Cottage. A reminder of time spent as a House Guide in another shrine inspired by the solace of nature.

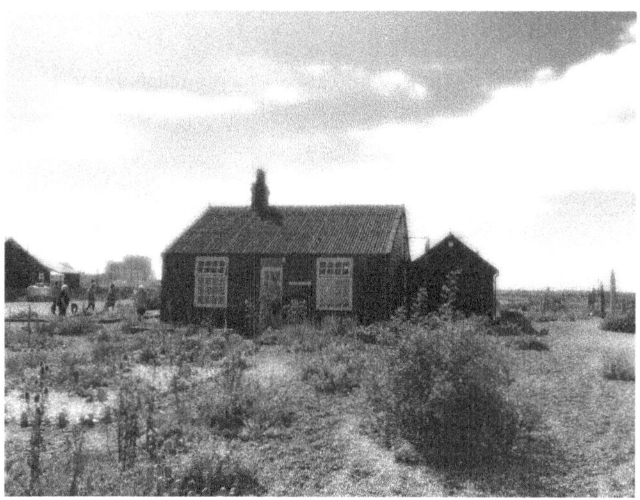

Prospect Cottage…The tiny fishermen's hut, black as pitch with daffodil yellow windows, the focal point of my pilgrimage and monument to the legacy of exile and creativity. From the opening page of *Modern Nature*, the inspirational diary that Jarman kept, 'there are no walls or fences here.' The bleak landscape of Dungeness, dreamily familiar and yet dislocated at the same time. Vast, empty and intense all at once. I tried to imagine what it would have been like living there at life's end with the lingering spectre of time past and passing. While present in every fold and drape of the landscape, the nuclear Camelot kept a silent watch moored in the firmament. An omnipresent ghost beached in the wilderness with a toxic haze that dazzles as it blows across the Ness. While the wind roared I walked entranced by a beach flooded with decaying boats, rusty engines and abandoned huts. A post-apocalyptic melancholy tinged with rust.

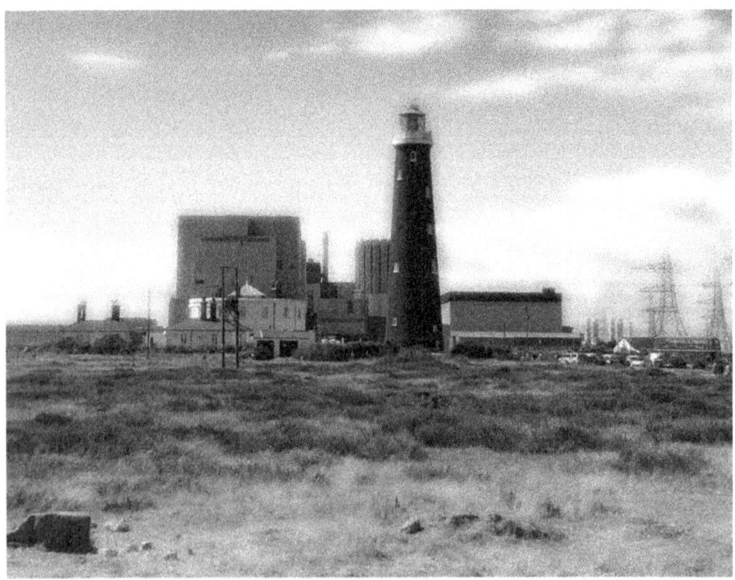

Approaching the cottage, I stood in front of a line of billowing washing with the loud peeping call of an oystercatcher rolling breathlessly over and over again. In the background Kent's mainline in miniature rumbled past on a 13.5 mile journey to Hythe. As expected the garden did not contain the symphony of colour so beautifully described in his journal. There weren't any traces of thundery teardrops or dewy peonies bent double or irises purple as the sky. Perished with the scalding sun, the loss of any scarlet poppies bursting with blue-black interiors was most keenly felt. Only a bare landscape parched from the recent heat wave sparkled in stripes of white sunlight. A stony desert where the strongest grasses thrive, predictably the sage green sea kale had taken hold. In stark contrast I thought back to late February when I left Manchester Art Gallery in monsoon-like conditions. Clasping on to four packets of wildflower seeds bought from the gallery shop that formed part of a set of products especially created for the exhibition *Derek Jarman Protest!*

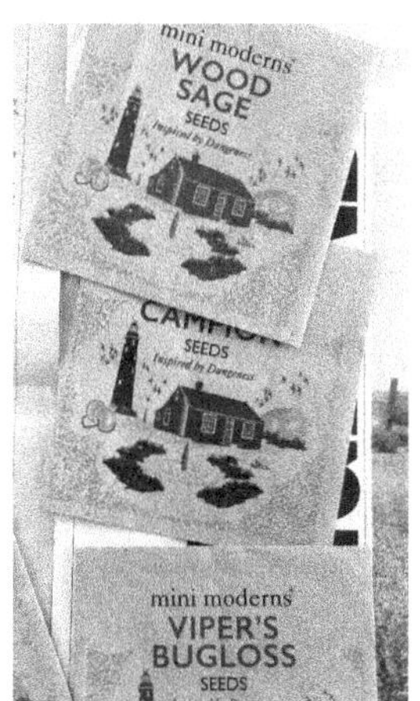

I remembered walking through the lockdown-delayed retrospective curated in loose chronological order by Jon Savage and Fiona Corridan. Where the avant-garde detritus of the great polymath's life served up a pageant of impulsive self-expression fused with creative wonder. Paintings, photographs, Super-8 music promos, film and general mixed media containing elements of barbed wire, glass, bone and coinage, combined with his work as a set designer, gardener and LGBTQ+/AIDS activist. The exhibition marked his fatal illness with a cabinet containing explanatory leaflets from the HIV and AIDS charity, the George House Trust. Another room showed the 1993 film *Blue*, a solitary cobalt screen and powerful symbol of Jarman's deteriorating eyesight as a result of AIDS-related sickness. I sat alone on a bench for a while listening to voices from the film swirling and circling before they disappeared back into the darkness.

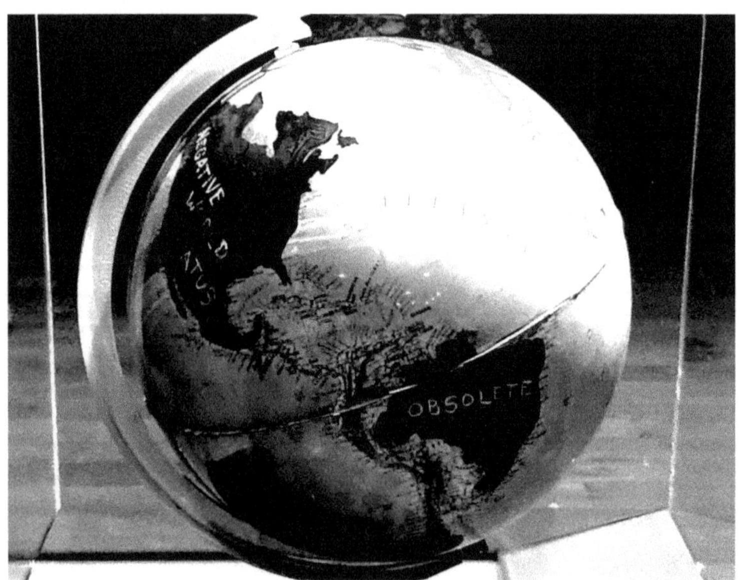

Opposite the globe from *Jubilee*, a restored print of his Super-8 film, *Jordan's Dance* played silently on a loop. The haunting mixture of power and pathos depicts a Swan Lake-style ballerina, scornfully pirouetting around a war torn landscape. Beside her a naked man wearing a golden theatrical mask stands next to a more sinister hooded figure. Both of them stare fixedly into a pile of burning rubbish that contains books draped in Union Jacks.

Notes: From Modern Nature Sunday 12th November
Jon Savage visits Jarman for a late lunch before they take a walk on the beach at Dungeness. They discuss Savage writing 55,000 words in one week for his 'punk book' along with events from the Silver Jubilee year. In particular, a humourless Vivienne Westwood dressed like a cross between Thatcher and Miss Jean Brodie appearing on the late Dame Edna show.

At 2.55pm I made my way to the front door framed with trademark yellow paint. At first nobody answered, so I trundled back and forth from front to back until I was eventually let in. A pair of smiling Creative Folkestone guides provided a warm greeting and ushered me into the hallway. Immediately a strong sense of claustrophobia gripped as I felt hemmed in by the dark, austere furniture. Once again I had flashbacks to the 'Houseplace' at Dove Cottage and the shadowy wooden panelling lit by a solitary candle. Where the words of Dorothy's journal glowed and often reduced visitors to reverent whispers, as they waited in the bruising black of the 19th century.

After another short wait in the hallway, it was obvious that the other people booked on the 3pm tour were not showing up. My guides, an older male somewhere in his mid-forties and a younger more effusive female began their opening spiel. I nodded along attentively and even offered a few experiences from my own short tenure guiding for the Wordsworth Trust. They seemed keen to share anecdotes.

"Sometimes people don't say a word and just walk round in silence with their heads bowed."

"Other times we've had relatives booked on who can get quite emotional!"

I smiled knowingly and tilted my head slightly to one side, "I used to get the occasional PhD student raising an eyebrow during my tours, especially whenever I tried to compare Wordsworth and Coleridge to Lennon and McCartney."

We laughed again and a friendly appreciation of how lucky we were in that precise moment spread throughout the spring room. I ambled gently stopping briefly to look out of a window framed perfectly by the sea. Crouching down, I leant over Jarman's writing desk, an 18th century elm table left brimming with several bottles of ink, pens, envelopes, scraps of paper and a small lead house that resembled Dorothy's in the Land of Oz. The guides sensing an opportunity instructed that his will had been left in a leather case on a stool next to the table. Sometimes they smiled warmly at each other, particularly when I looked at an Italian public health poster; "It's Easy to Save a Life" that featured a photograph of two guys kissing. A Dungeness resident for a number of years, I thought the older guide probably knew more than I could imagine. Doors to the four rooms had been left open with salt rosary beads hanging over the entrance to the bedroom. In the studio I stood on thick blobs of paint surrounding a workbench guarded by a pair of steel toe capped boots. A set of royal blue fisherman's overalls hung in a corner beside a display cabinet exhibiting a trademark Super-8 camera. Directly opposite, heavy shelves overflowed with a selection of books from Jarman's library. Amongst many familiar names: Goya, Schwitters and Gilbert and George stood out.

Notes: From Modern Nature Tuesday 6th June 1989
Jarman dismisses what he calls Gilbert and George's constrictive values as the language of loutish conservative youths out on macho stag nights. However, he does express a love for their paintings and admires the way they put themselves in the centre of their art at a time when many artists chose to remain anonymous.

In the hallway several film stills and a Richard Hamilton original hung closely together. As we made a right turn into the sun room the intense dark clouds of claustrophobia lifted immediately. Entering a lighter and roomier extension (often used for entertaining) a set of large open windows opened out onto the wasteland with views across to the haunting power station. Suddenly the outsider's refuge turned into a glass box conservatory with a light beige armchair to match. According to the guides HB used to put on loud grime music to try and ward off prospectors. (HB – the 'Hinney Beast' was the nickname given to Jarman's partner Keith Collins, whom he bequeathed Prospect Cottage to until his own death in 2018).

After nearly an hour trying to make sense of the furnishings and items on display I said my goodbyes and exited back through the front door. Outside into Jarman's forest of impenetrable thorns festooned with driftwood, stone circles and various sticks with bits of flotsam scavenged from daily beach combing duties. In the late afternoon sunshine the garden had fallen silent and perfectly solitary. A magical scene worthy of a fading white witch crunching softly across the shingle dressed in a trademark hooded djellaba.

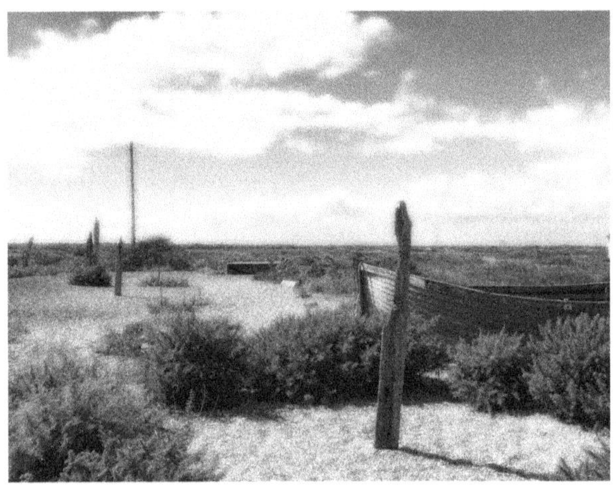

Notes: *Djellaba — Jarman often used to wear a djellaba or jillaba (also written gallabea) - a long, loose-fitted unisex outer robe or dress with full sleeves worn every day in the Maghreb region of North Africa. They are designed to protect the wearer from the desert sun and cold nights. When he started to make his garden at Prospect Cottage local fishermen believed something of the occult was taking place. Using totems made out of driftwood combined with a series of stone circles, Jarman remarked at the time, 'People thought I was building a garden for magical purposes,' some of them assumed he was a white witch out to get the nuclear power station…*

I walked along Battery Road past signs advertising fresh bait and local fish from the Pilot Inn. The very place where it had all began an abandoned search for bluebell woods that led to the discovery of modern nature. 'There's a beautiful fisherman's cottage here, and if ever it was for sale I think I'd buy it,' Jarman memorably remarked to HB on the drive through Kent that ended with a detour to get fish and chips. There with a green and white 'For Sale' sign outside. He made an offer for Prospect Cottage on the spot and the rest is history. Sited in a scattered community of fishermen's cottages, Jarman was certainly not isolated. Despite fears that something supernatural might be taking place he was welcomed into the community and embraced it in equal measure.

With the familiar sound of stones crunching underfoot I strode out on the vast expanse of longshore drift toward the automated lighthouse painted in thick bands of black and white. The fifth on the Ness, it began operation in 1961 after light from its predecessor became obscured by the new nuclear power station. I holed up at the Britannia inn with a ringside view of the two lighthouses adjacent to the end of the miniature railway line. Over a pint I returned to a small section from Olivia Laing's introduction to *Modern Nature* – where England's losses are bound to the soul of melancholy in a diary punctuated by dreams of the dead…Opening a window, I observed a Shepherd Neame pub sign blowing back and forth in the breeze. Everything fell silent for a second or two, while in my mind's eye I substituted the usual female warrior image with that of a high priestess of punk. A final resplendent fantasy rocking a sheer Union Jack vest, green stockings and suspenders with a burlesque feather fan. The white lip clanking of fishing boats masked in clouds of herring gulls marked a return from the sea and woke me from the reverie. As the last of England's golden summer light faded and cast shadows that caressed the shore, it had been a long, hot memorable day. Even in deathly silence, the self-titled 'hermit in the wilderness of illness' still dominates the shingle.

Yes, I thought, I have had my vision…